Traditio.
Blackwork Samplers

To Joyce Bull and Mary Ticehurst.

Traditional
Blackwork Samplers

Lesley Wilkins

SEARCH PRESS

First published in Great Britain 2004

Search Press Limited
Wellwood, North Farm Road,
Tunbridge Wells, Kent TN2 3DR

Text copyright © Lesley Wilkins 2004
Embroidery designs copyright © Lesley Wilkins 2004

Photographs by Jon Firth and Charlotte de la Bédoyère,
Search Press Studios
Photographs and design copyright © Search Press Ltd 2004

ISBN 1 84448 022 4

The Publishers and author can accept no responsibility for any
consequences arising from the information, advice or instructions
given in this publication.

Readers are permitted to reproduce any of the items/patterns in
this book for their personal use, or for the purposes of selling for
charity, free of charge and without the prior permission of the
Publishers. Any use of the items/patterns for commercial purposes
is not permitted without the prior permission of the Publishers.

Suppliers
If you have difficulty in obtaining any of the materials and
equipment mentioned in this book, then please write to the
Publishers, at the address above, for a current list of stockists,
including firms who operate a mail-order service.

Acknowledgements
*The Publisher would like to thank the
V & A Picture Library for permission to reproduce the
Jane Bostocke embroidery on page 9 and Mary Evans
Picture Library for the picture on pages 24–25.
Special thanks to Elizabeth Mason for her kind
permission to use the picture on pages 46–47 and for
her trouble in sending it to us.*

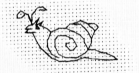

Publisher's note
All the step-by-step photographs in this book feature the
author, Lesley Wilkins, demonstrating blackwork
embroidery. No models have been used.

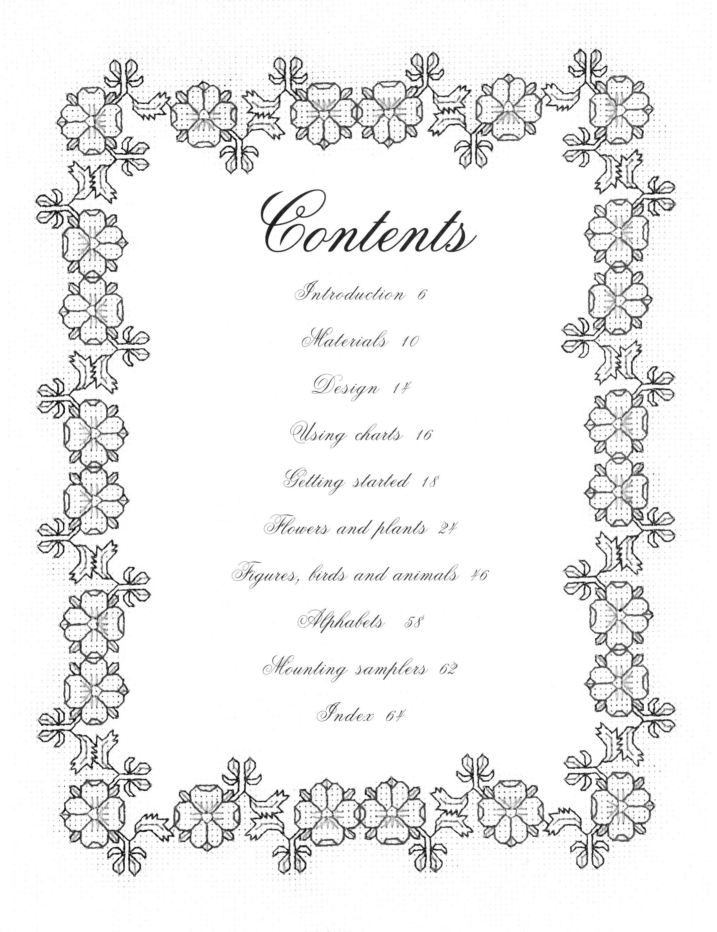

Contents

Introduction

Before the advent of printed pattern books, band samplers were a means of recording the embroidery patterns used for decorating household linens and clothing. The first book of embroidery patterns was printed by Johann Sibmacher in Augsburg, Germany in 1523, but it was not until over fifty years later in 1587 that the first English pattern book appeared.

Before this time, new stitches and patterns were eagerly collected and exchanged between friends by adding them to a sampler before the pattern was forgotten. The strips of embroidery could be rolled up and carried in a work bag and loaned to fellow embroiderers.

The traditional band sampler, sometimes known as a long sampler because of its long, narrow shape, is particularly associated with English embroidery from the sixteenth and seventeenth centuries. Worked on narrow strips of plain-weave linen, some of which measured up to 101cm (40in), the band sampler was the perfect way to record embroidered border patterns, most of which were based on repeating motifs.

The introduction of blackwork to England is usually attributed to the arrival of Katharine of Aragon in 1501 from Spain, but examples existed before she arrived. The patterns are greatly influenced by Moorish style and the geometric patterns used in Spain for centuries. One of the main stitches used, running stitch, was firstly named Spanish stitch, and later became known as 'blackwork' after Katharine's divorce from Henry VIII in 1533, when all things Spanish fell from favour. It was also named Holbein stitch after the Tudor court painter Hans Holbein, whose subjects wore clothes decorated in blackwork. Thankfully his paintings record many of the patterns used on clothing, because not many pieces of stitched work survive from this period.

Opposite

A variety of framed band samplers. These were inspired by those made by embroiderers of the past who recorded numerous patterns on cloth before pattern books were available.

Patterns which were printed for lace-making during the Renaissance period showed linear designs that could be adapted for blackwork, and also provided ideas for other types of embroidery. The formal garden designs of the Tudor period were another source of inspiration, particularly the elaborate knot gardens, which took the form of interlacing bands and abstract patterns containing coloured sands, gravels or plants marked out and framed by low hedges.

One of the oldest surviving blackwork samplers, dated 1598, was worked by Jane Bostocke, and is kept in the Victoria and Albert Museum in London. There are many blackwork patterns recorded on this sampler, and they have been used throughout the designs in this book.

The samplers in this book should prove a useful source of reference for embroiderers. The patterns that appear are traditional designs dating from up to five centuries ago. I hope that you will enjoy working the projects and that they will inspire you further to design your own.

Opposite

This sampler by Jane Bostocke is one of the earliest known, dated at 1598, and was worked with metallic threads, silks, pearls and beads in a variety of stitches. The random disposition of the motifs and various patterns showed that Jane Bostocke added to her sampler whenever a new pattern was found. On the original sampler, which is now in the Victoria and Albert Museum in London, there are twenty-four different border designs and several naturalistic spot motifs. This shows how early samplers were used as a reference resource.

Materials

Fabric

Blackwork requires fabric that is woven evenly in blocks or with a specific number of threads to the inch. Some of the patterns can be very intricate and therefore require a fabric that has a smaller block count to the inch, or a finer thread.

There is a great variety of different fabric and thread colours available. If you are creating a sampler that you want to look aged when it is completed, use off-whites such as antique white, rustico or oatmeal shades in Aida. Unbleached or old white linens also give the work an aged feel. The success of a blackwork design depends on a strong contrast between the fabric and the thread so whatever your colour, choose the thread carefully so that the pattern stands out clearly. With all the variables available to the blackwork embroiderer: in the thickness of the thread, the pattern density and the weight of the fabric, there is not always a need for much colour to create impact.

Aida (block weave)

This is a cotton or cotton mixture fabric and is very practical for counted needlework. It is available in a variety of colours and block counts, with two threads woven into blocks rather than a single thread. It gives accurate results and is ideal for the beginner. The majority of the designs in this book are worked on this fabric.

Evenweave

A plain, single weave fabric with the number of threads for the warp and weft being exactly the same. As the texture is open, the threads are easy to count.

Hardanger

This has pairs of intersecting threads and is easy to count. It is slightly more practical than Evenweave as it keeps its shape more firmly.

Needles

Tapestry needles, which are blunt, are required for blackwork. They range from size 26 to the finest, size 14. The type of thread you use determines the size of the needle. The needle needs to go through the fabric without distorting the hole in any way; sizes 22–26 are usually best.

Threads

Silk threads were originally used centuries ago, but only by the rich. Now of course, silk threads are available to everyone and there is a greater choice.

Stranded cotton

This is the most popular thread, and the most suitable for blackwork. It has six strands and can be used in many different thicknesses, depending on how many strands are used.

Perle cottons

These come in a variety of thicknesses, from the finest, no. 12 to the thickest, no. 3. An ideal thread for blackwork, with a sheen effect, it is good for outlining.

Coton à broder

This comes in several thicknesses, 40 being the finest and 8 the thickest. It is good for outlining and sits very well on the fabric.

Cotton perle 5 and 8, coton à broder 16, stranded cotton and ordinary machine cotton, gold lamé and mouline metallise threads with needles in sizes 22, 24 and 26. The fabrics shown are Aida, Evenweave and Hardanger in decorative strips and larger cuts.

Frames

There are a variety of types to choose from, depending on the size of your fabric. Freestanding frames can now take clip-on magnifiers and lamps, which enable you to have both hands free to sew. Whatever frame you use, the important rule is: always make sure the fabric is drum-tight.

Hoops

These frames are suitable only when the whole of the design fits within the ring area, as stitches can become distorted if you have to move the ring around as you work. The fabric is attached by placing it over the smaller hoop, then forcing the larger hoop over it. The screw should then be tightened to secure the fabric.

Rectangular frame

This frame can accommodate the whole of the fabric width and you can keep the fabric taut throughout by rolling the fabric to the required area and tightening the screws at each corner.

A selection of hand-held rectangular frames and hoops and a seated frame, which allows you to work with both hands free. The clip-on magnifier provides a clearer view for close, intricate patterns. I do not like to work by artificial light, so I always set myself up beside a window.

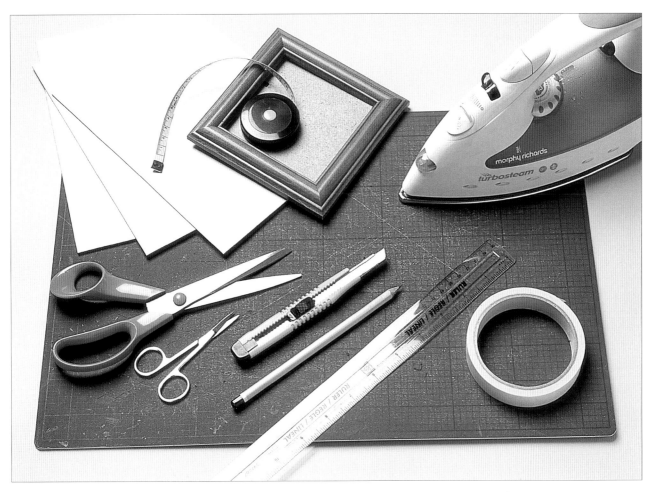

Other items

A cutting mat, mounting board, picture frame, tape measure, iron, masking tape, ruler, pencil, craft knife, embroidery scissors and dressmaker's scissors.

Embroidery scissors These should be kept sharp to cut the thread in one motion, and the points are useful to unpick mistakes, so they should be fine enough to slip under the stitch and cut it safely.

Dressmaker's scissors To cut the fabric. Always follow the line of the thread to ensure a straight cut.

Tape measure or ruler For choosing fabric size and again when the finished work is to be mounted.

Iron Used to press the finished work before it is mounted.

Pins Used to mark the centre of the fabric before you begin sewing, and to attach the fabric to the edge of the mounting board to keep it in place when lacing or taping the back.

Cutting mat and craft knife These are essential when cutting mounting board.

Acid-free mounting board This is used when mounting your samplers.

Masking tape This prevents the fabric edge from fraying.

Double-sided tape Useful when mounting your finished work.

Picture frame A good frame is the perfect finishing touch for a sampler. The glass can be left in the frame to protect the work from dust, but to prevent the stitches being flattened by the glass, use a card border to rest the glass on or a strip of acid-free mounting board around the inside edge of the frame.

Design

Blackwork is a very creative and flexible form of stitching, made up of straight or diagonal stitches arranged in a huge variety of patterns. There are numerous traditional patterns to be found in books, but it can be fascinating to create your own. Centuries ago, people were influenced by what they saw in their surroundings. Pattern books were not available until the sixteenth century, which is why the band sampler was created, so that people could keep a record of their designs.

Moorish and Arab craftsmen favoured geometric motifs and all-over patterning, which can be found on doorways, mosaic tiles, architecture and other crafts. When these craftsmen became a dominant force in Spain, they influenced the textiles of the country with designs based on grape vines, leaves, roses, pomegranates, heraldic griffins and lions. These motifs, collected over the centuries, were embroidered in black silk on white linen, and were called 'Spanishwork', which was later changed to 'blackwork'.

Ideas for patterns can be found wherever you travel if you look at the buildings that surround you, or even in a simple tile design book. I collect pictures based on a particular subject, such as Tudor knot gardens and mazes which inspired embroiderers of the Renaissance period, and from these I create my own patterns.

I collected pictures of Tudor knot gardens, which provide design ideas from their intricate, interlocking patterns, and also Moorish tiles, which inspired blackwork of the Renaissance period. Designs inspired by these pictures were then transferred to graph paper.

Pattern density

Light and dark areas can be created in a design by varying the density of the pattern. Closely worked, dense areas of pattern look darker, but if you eliminate parts of the pattern and open it out, that area will look lighter.

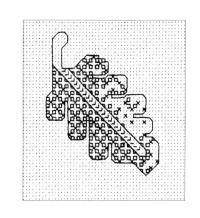

Thread thickness

The more strands of thread you use, the darker and more prominent the design appears.

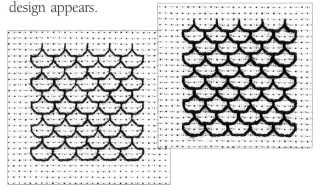

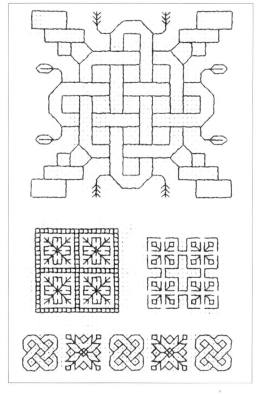

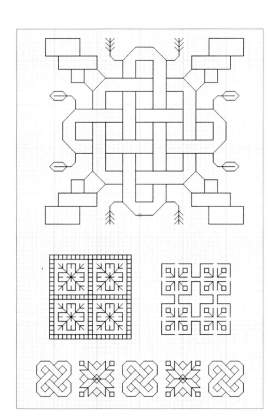

Working from the sketches opposite, I created the chart and finally the blackwork sampler shown above. The design at the top echoes the shape of the low-cut hedges which formed knot gardens and mazes. The square Moorish tile design is built up from single motifs on the bottom line, and repeat patterns in the middle.

Using charts

The first stitch you place in the fabric when you begin your project can be vital to its success. If you start sewing in the wrong area, you may find halfway through that you have run out of space, and hours of work have been wasted.

On any chart there should be a grey square or black cross to indicate the centre of the design. You can find the centre of your fabric by folding it into four, and this should correspond with the centre mark on the chart.

The chart for the embroidery below is shown opposite. The centre marker can be found below the main flower head. The flower motif is to be sewn first, and this in turn will help you to position the surrounding patterns. One strand of thread has been used throughout the design, but with a variety of colours used to distinguish between the different flower motifs.

A colourful design featuring fuchsias, roses and acorns, inspired by pot displays and pictures in gardening books.

Design size: 8 x 7cm (3¹/₈ x 2¾in)
Fabric: Aida 16 count, antique white
Threads: DMC Green 904
          Pink 3350
          Mauve 552
          Yellow 742
          Brown 801
Use one strand throughout

Getting started

Choosing fabric

When the design is ready to be sewn, choose your fabric carefully and make sure the measurements are correct before cutting the fabric to the required size. Include 10–15cm (4–6in) extra fabric around the design to allow for stretching and mounting. Smaller projects do not require as much.

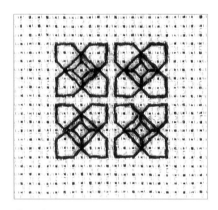

Aida

The fabric is constructed in blocks and this makes counting easier, especially for the beginner. It is available in 8, 14, 18 and 22 count. It prevents the stitches from becoming uneven and gives a neater, crisper end result to your work.

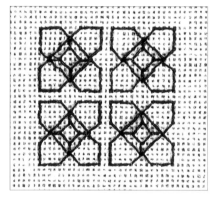

Evenweave

This is stitched over two threads and lends itself well to counted embroidery, though it requires more concentration.

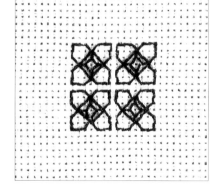

Hardanger

The fabric is made up of pairs of threads which are woven together to give a denser background, but the holes are easily visible between the warp and weft.

Framing

Rectangular frames are more practical for larger projects as they keep the fabric taut at all times and prevent the work from becoming distorted. If the fabric frays easily, it can be edged with masking tape before you attach it to the frame.

1. To find the centre of the fabric, fold it in half, then in half again the other way. Mark the centre point with a pin.

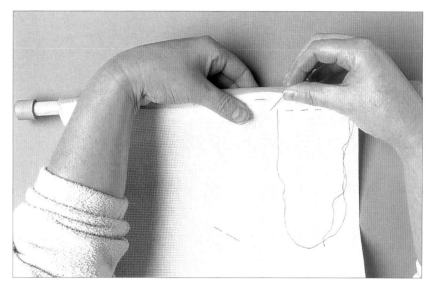

2. Use a frame wide enough to take the width of the fabric and sew the fabric to the webbing on the rollers using running stitch.

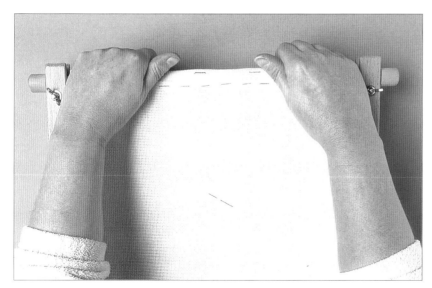

3. Attach the rollers to the frame and roll the fabric until it is taut. Screw the bolts tight to keep the fabric in place.

Stitches

The most common stitches used in blackwork are double running stitch, back stitch and cross stitch. All the projects in this book can be worked using these three stitches.

Double running stitch

Also known as Holbein stitch, this provides a smoother appearance than back stitch and is ideal for intricate geometric patterns.

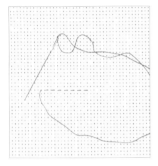

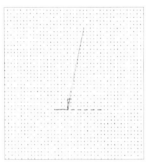

1. Sew a line of running stitches.

2. Go back along the same line filling in the spaces between the stitches.

A finished example of double running stitch.

Back stitch

This is used for outlining other stitches as well as in its own right. It gives definition to the design, especially when you are using thicker thread or more than one strand.

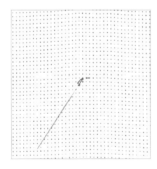

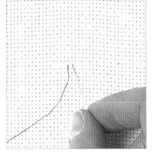

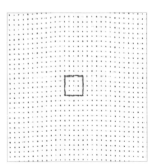

1. Bring the needle up to the right side of the fabric, then take it down to the wrong side at the next point.

2. At the front of the first stitch, bring the needle up to the right side of the fabric again.

3. Finish the stitch by inserting the needle at the point where the last stitch began.

A finished example of back stitch.

Cross stitch

This is the most commonly used counted stitch and is ideal for a variety of patterns and designs. To ensure its neatness, always make sure the top stitch in each cross faces in the same direction.

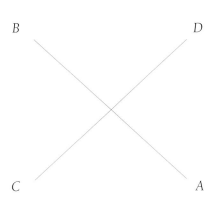

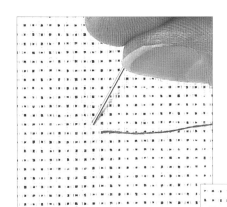

1. Begin at point A. Bring the needle up to the right side of the fabric and insert the needle diagonally at point B.

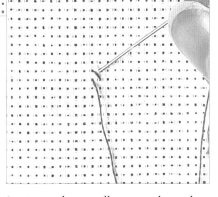

2. Bring the needle up to the right side of the fabric at point C and insert it down diagonally at point D. For the next stitch, bring the needle up at point C and repeat the procedure.

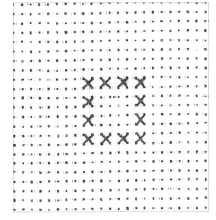

A finished example of cross stitch.

Starting your design

It is always the safest option to start at the centre of your design, and this will ensure that an adequate margin surrounds it. The chart you work from usually has a grey square or cross to indicate the centre.

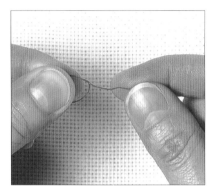

1. Make a knot at the end of the thread. This is called the waste knot and will be removed later when the end is secured.

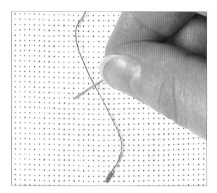

2. Insert the needle from the right side of the work into an area, not far from the starting point, that will eventually be covered by stitch work. These stitches will secure the end of the thread.

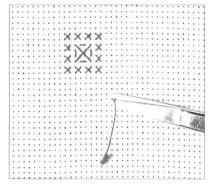

3. The thread where you began sewing should now be secure at the back, as the pattern has covered it. Cut off the waste knot and continue with your design.

Finishing off

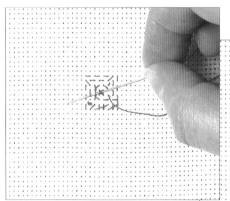

1. On the wrong side of the work, finish a thread by catching two or three stitches underneath. Make sure you do not surface on the right side of the work.

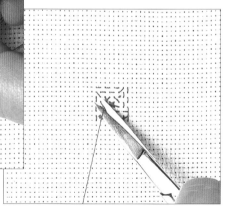

2. Cut off any loose ends with sharp embroidery scissors.

In this framed embroidery, the strawberries were worked in cross stitch, using gold metallic thread. The outline was back stitch and all other parts of the design were worked in double running stitch. If the embroidery has been started and finished as shown, with no knots and no loose threads at the back, it should sit flat when mounted and framed.

Flowers and plants

Part of the charm of Elizabethan gardens was in the complexity of mazes used for the sport and amusement of the lord and his guests. The intricate patterns were duplicated in embroidery with twisting vines and stems leading to different parts of the design and revealing new patterns. Sometimes the designs for entire gardens were worked into larger embroideries for cushions, bed hangings and wall tapestries. Individual plants also inspired designs for blackwork, and roses, pansies, honeysuckle, carnations, violets, strawberries, pomegranates, grapevines and acorns were carefully stitched on to garments and furnishings, recording Elizabethan gardens at the height of their splendour. The rose was the national flower of England, and was among the most popular of all blackwork motifs. Pomegranates, a pagan symbol of fertility, were particularly associated with Katharine of Aragon who popularised blackwork in England, and this was another favourite motif.

The interlocking patterns of Elizabethan knot gardens and mazes inspired many blackwork designs, as did the flowers, fruits and nuts found in those gardens.

24

This band sampler contains ten examples of patterns that appear on the Jane Bostocke sampler shown on page 9. It is worked in black and gold threads.

Design size: 31 x 61.7cm (12¼ x 24¼in)

Fabric: Aida 18 count, antique white

Threads: DMC Black 310 (6)
         DMC Gold 5282 (1)

Use one strand of black and two strands of gold thread

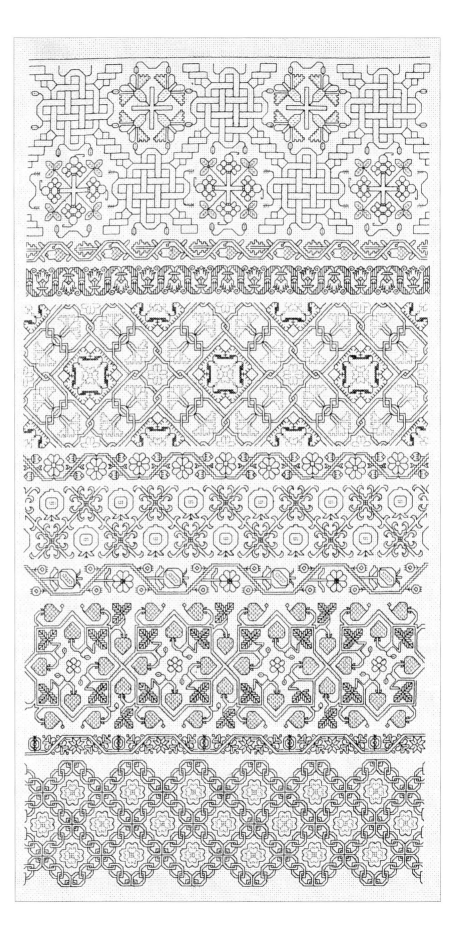

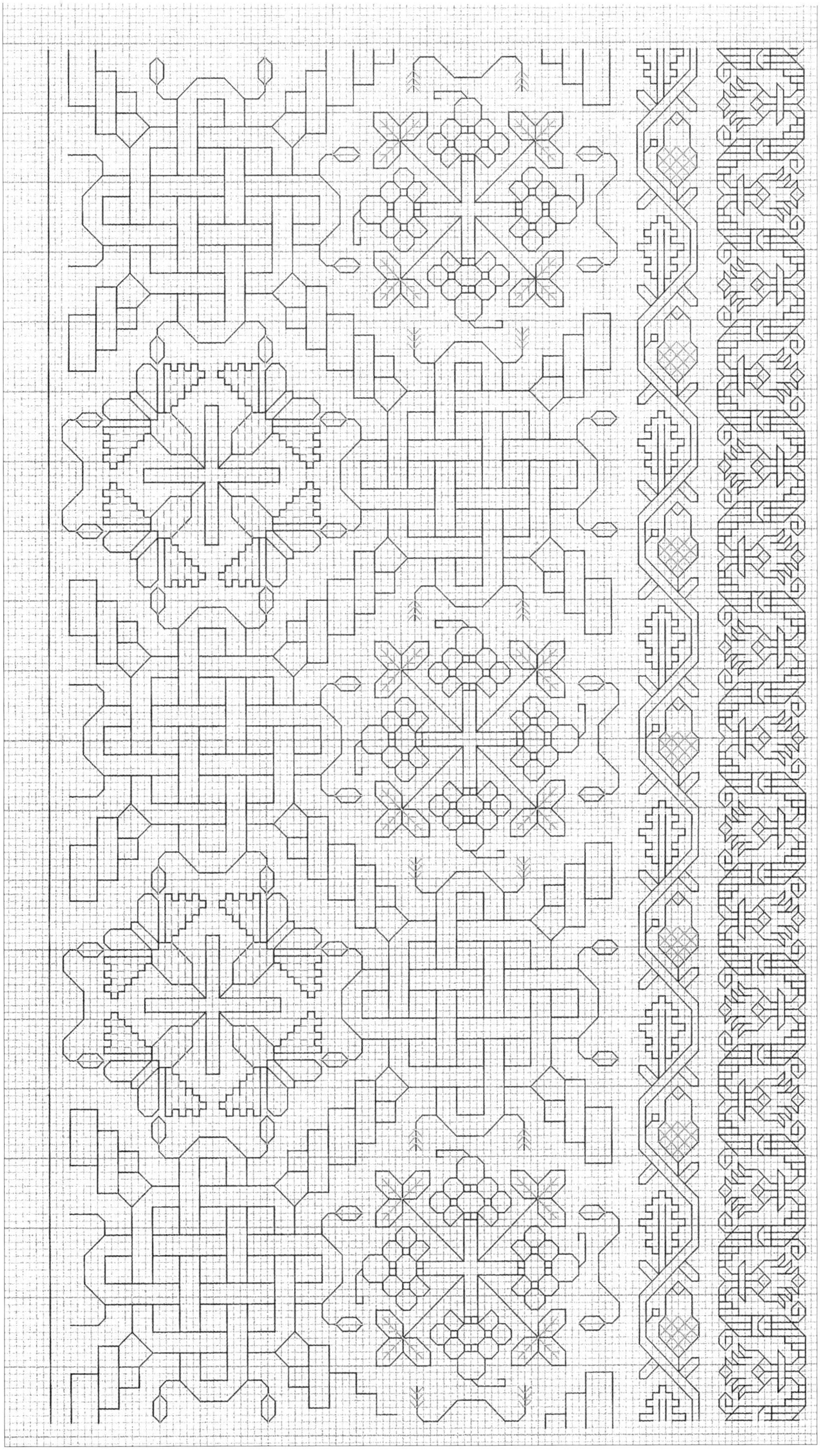

Chart for the top of the embroidery – this way up

Chart for the middle of the embroidery – this way up

Chart for the bottom of the embroidery – this way up

This sampler was inspired by the pattern layouts of Elizabethan gardens with their mazes and knot gardens, surrounded by roses and grapevines.

Design size: 15 x 40cm (5⅞ x 15¾in)
Fabric: Aida 16 count, antique white
Thread: DMC Black 310 (2)
Use one strand throughout

31

This blue sampler is built up from repeat patterns, many of which were used in household furnishings.

Design size: 28.5 x 47.5cm
(11¼ x 18¾in)
Fabric: Aida 16 count, antique white
Thread: DMC blue 336 (3)
Use one strand throughout

Chart for the top of the embroidery – this way up

Chart for the middle of the embroidery – this way up

Chart for the bottom of the embroidery – this way up

Once again, the main theme
of this sampler is flowers,
especially honeysuckle
and roses.

Design size: 28.5 x 47.5cm
(11¼ x 18¾in)
Fabric: Aida 16 count,
        antique white
Thread: DMC Dark
Red 815 (3)
Use one strand throughout

37

Chart for the middle of the embroidery – this way up

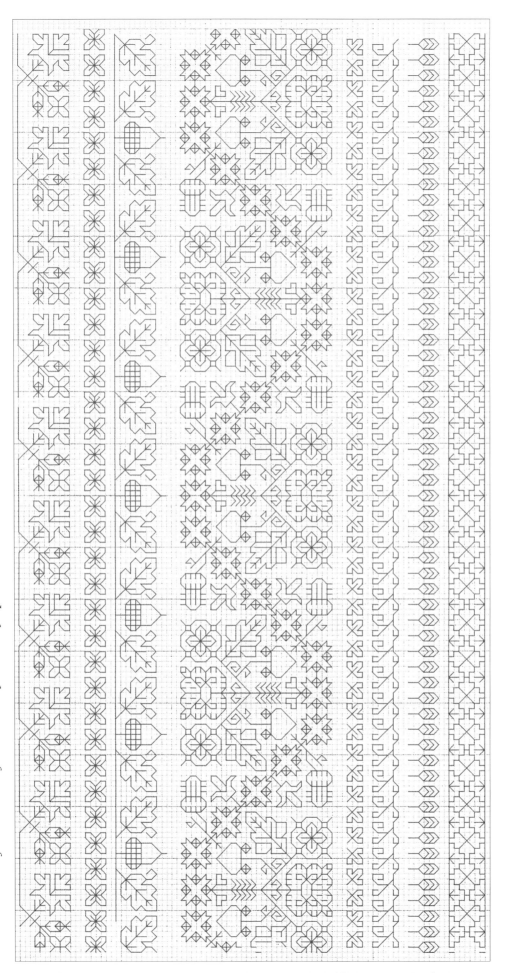

Chart for the bottom of the embroidery – this way up

Flower and plant borders

Flowers and plants found in everyday surroundings were a popular theme in blackwork borders, which were used on household furnishings as well as clothing.

Border designs featuring flowers, thistles, acorns and knotwork shapes are combined in this band sampler.

Design size:
16.5 x 24.5cm (6½ x 9⅝in)
Fabric: Aida 16 count, antique white
Thread:
DMC Dark Pink 3350 (1)
Orange 3776 (1)
Light Green 470 (1)
Dark Green 986 (1)
Mauve 553 (1)
Brown 801 (1)

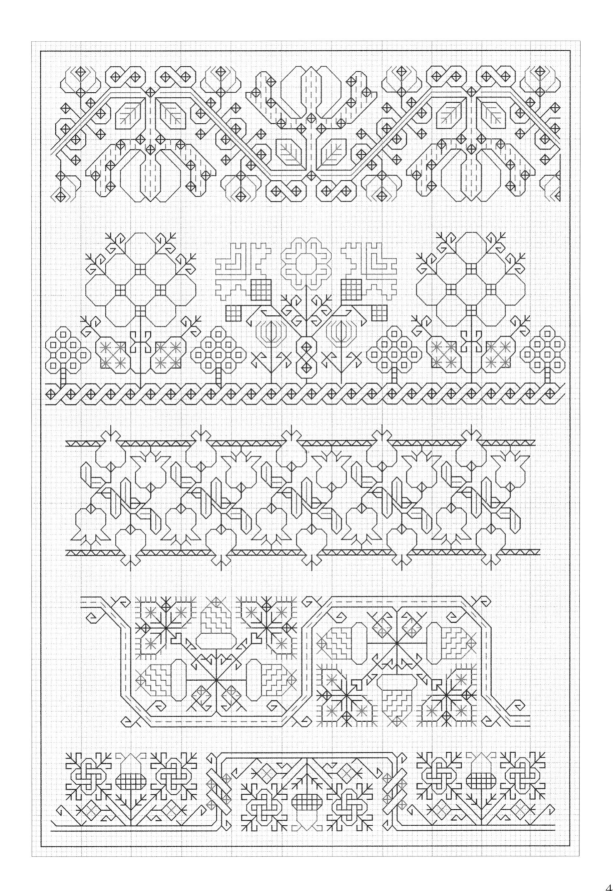

41

*A variety of flowers including the iris,
artichoke and pansy appear in this sampler.
Design size: 17 x 21cm (6¾ x 8¼in)
Fabric: Aida 16 count, antique white
Thread: DMC Light Pink 3733 (1)*

*Dark Pink 3350 (1)
Orange 3776 (1)
Light Green 470 (1)
Dark Green 986 (1)
Mauve 553 (1)
Blue 780 (1)*

43

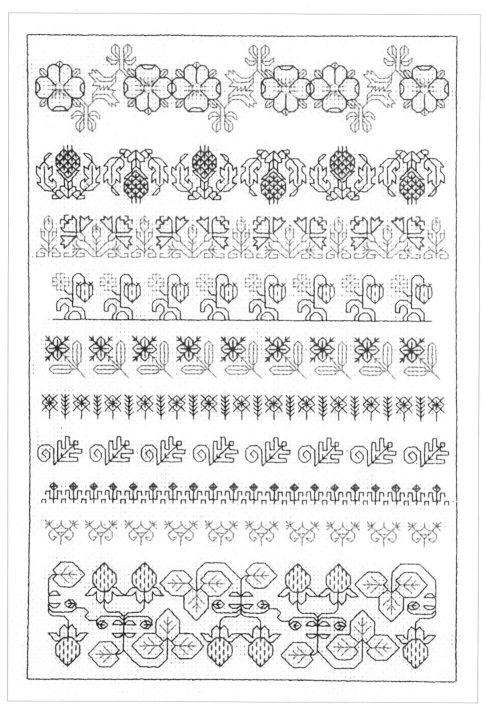

Smaller borders like these were originally used on the edges of clothing, such as on the cuffs, to provide extra reinforcement.

Design size: 16.5 x 24cm (6½ x 9½in)

Fabric: Aida 16 count, antique white

Thread: DMC Light Pink 3733 (1)

Dark Pink 3350 (1)
Orange 3776 (1)
Light Green 470 (1)
Dark Green 986 (1)
Mauve 553 (1)

45

Figures, birds and animals

By the end of the sixteenth century, books were becoming available, and they served as pattern sources for the embroiderer. This source became an important factor for the character and development of Elizabethan embroidery. The books covered subjects such as natural history, botanical and herbal, and the exotic plants, animals and birds that were being encountered by explorers of the New World. Creatures such as monkeys, camels, parrots, elephants and crocodiles began to appear in embroideries, as well as mythical creatures like the phoenix and the unicorn. Other sources such as wallpaper books and woodcut patterns for printing were also used for ideas by the embroiderer. Designs were transferred from the book to the fabric by punching tiny holes in the printed page, following the outline of the shape. The page was then placed on to the fabric and dusted with charcoal to produce a dotted outline. This technique was known as pouncing, and is one reason why so few of these early source books for embroidery designs have survived.

Figures were not used as much as birds and animals. Most of them, it is believed, had a symbolic meaning, such as the boxer or, as it was sometimes called, the lover or Renaissance Cupid. This figure often appears to be holding something such as a flower in its hand, as though bearing a gift.

This page of designs comes from A Schole House For The Needle, *published in 1632 by Richard Shorleyker. Bought in a rummage sale for a few pence in the 1940s, this book turned out to be of great interest to historians, since so few books of its kind have survived. Its title page states: 'Here followeth certaine patternes of cut-workes. Also sundry sorts of Spots, as Flowers, Birds and Fishes etc. and will fitly serve to be wrought, some with Gould, some with Silke and some with Crewll, or otherwise as your pleasure'.*

This sampler includes many commonplace English items such as goats, ducks and acorns, as well as a human figure who may have represented Adam.

Design size: 11.5 x 24cm (4½ x 9½in)
Fabric: Aida 16 count, antique white
Threads: DMC Green 501
            Orange 3776
            Yellow 742
            Pink 3726
            Brown 839
            Blue 931
Use one strand throughout

Figures like the ones shown here are sometimes known as 'boxers' because of their stance. They were worked in back stitch or running stitch. They were often shown carrying acorns, flowers or heart-shaped objects, which may have suggested that they were bearing gifts. These figures have also been referred to as Cupids.

Design size: 10.7 x 7.7cm
(4¼ x 3in)

Fabric: Aida 16 count,
        antique white

Thread: DMC Black 315 (1)
            Gold 5282 (1)

Some people believe that pairs of figures like these represented Adam and Eve. These two are certainly in a beautiful garden!

Design size: 11.5 x 6.5cm
(4½ x 2⅝in)

Fabric: Aida 16 count, antique white

Thread: DMC Grey 414 (1)
        Pink 3350 (1)
        Green 986 (1)
        Dark Brown 839 (1)
        Light Brown 783 (1)
        Orange 3776 (1)
        Gold 5282 (1)

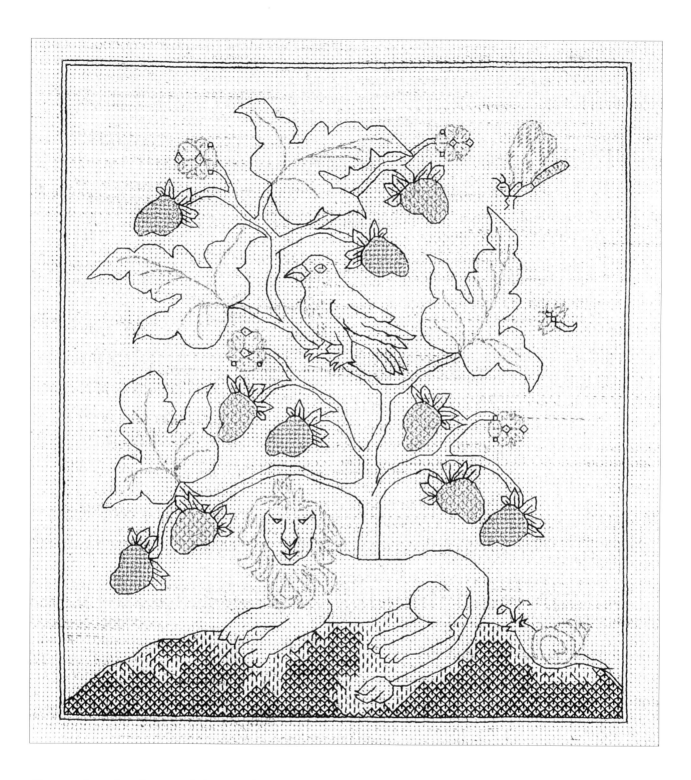

This sampler is based on motifs from woodcut illustrations.

Design size: 18.5 x 20.5cm (7¼ x 8⅛in)

Fabric: Aida 16 count, chino

Thread: DMC Brown 839 (1)
Gold 5282 (1)

A variety of insects and small animals which would have been traced from available books, or inspired directly by the contents of the garden.

Design size: 16.5 x 24cm (6½ x 9½in)
Fabric: Aida 16 count, antique white
Threads: DMC Black 310 (1)

The outlines of the designs were sewn using back stitch.
Design size: 16 x 24.5cm (6¼ x 9⅝in)

Fabric: Aida 16 count, antique white
Thread: DMC Black 310 (1)

Alphabets

Alphabets were not a great feature of blackwork embroidery, except for the marking of household linen, but they became more popular towards the seventeenth century, when they were used for schoolroom purposes.

On many of the samplers the letters I, J, U, V and W were omitted. This may have been because the Latin alphabet left out J, V and W. V was the capital form of U and J was not used until the mid-nineteenth century. J evolved from the letter I, which had appeared in the fourteenth century and was still used only occasionally during the sixteenth.

The letters from this sampler can also be used individually, to adorn a small object such as a pincushion.

Design size: 22 x 27.3cm (8⅝ x 10¾in)
Fabric: Aida 18 count, Chino
Thread: DMC Brown 801 (1) Gold 5282 (1)

Less ornate letters and numbers like these were used mainly for the marking of household linen.

Design size: 13.5 x 19.7cm (5³⁄₈ x 7³⁄₄in)

Fabric: Aida 16 count, antique white
Thread: DMC Black 310 (1)
Pink 3350 (1)

ABCDEFGHIJKLMNOPQR
STUVWXYZ
abcdefghijklmnopqrstuvwxyz
1234567890
ABCDEFGHIJKLMNOPQRSTUVWXYZ
1234567890
ABCDEFGHIJKLM
NOPQRSTUVWXYZ
abcdefghijklmnopqrstuvwxyz
1234567890
ABCDEFGHIJKLMN
OPQRSTUVWXYZ
1234567890

Mounting samplers

It is always worth finishing your work properly by stretching and mounting the fabric. Always use an acid-free mounting board to protect the fabric from discolouration. The way in which your design is framed can have a great influence on the way it will finally look, so take time over framing your work.

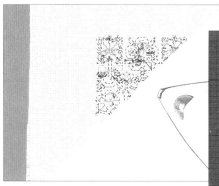

1. Place the embroidery face down and cover it with a fine, dry cloth. Iron it gently with a warm iron to avoid flattening the stitches.

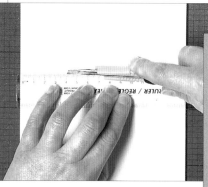

2. Cut the mounting board to the size you need, using a cutting mat and a craft knife.

3. Find the centre of the cut mounting board and push a needle into the board to mark the spot.

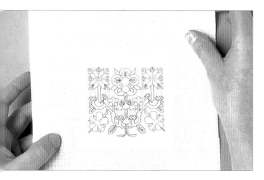

4. Measure the embroidery to find the centre point and push this point over the eye of the needle on to the board. This will ensure that the embroidery is positioned centrally on the mounting board.

5. Place pins through the fabric at the board's edges. Push them in horizontally so that the board can be turned over easily.

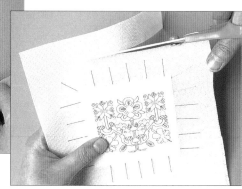

6. Trim the excess fabric to about 5cm (2in) all round and turn the embroidery over.

7. To mitre the corners, fold down the fabric corners, then fold in the sides and pin them down.

8. Sew the fabric edges together at the corners, and when secure, remove the pins.

9. The straight edges of the fabric can then be secured with masking tape.

10. The mounted embroidery is then ready to be placed into the frame, ready for display.

The work mounted and framed. Properly done, it will sit proudly on the wall for display.

Index